Preparing the Environment for Worship

David McNorgan

NOVALIS

THE LITURGICAL PRESS

Design: Eye-to-Eye Design, Toronto

Layout: Suzanne Latourelle

Illustrations: Eugene Kral

Series Editor: Bernadette Gasslein

© 1997, Novalis, Saint Paul University, Ottawa, Ontario, Canada

Business Office: Novalis, 49 Front Street East, 2nd floor, Toronto, Ontario M5E 1B3

Novalis: ISBN 2 89088 797 9

The Liturgical Press: ISBN 0-8146-2443-X
A Liturgical Press Book
Published in the United States of America by The Liturgical Press, Box 7500, Collegeville, MN 56321-7500

Illustrations on the following pages are based on slides taken by the author at:
P.4, 21, 33   St. Basil's Church, Ottawa
p. 26, 38, 40 Chapel of Mary, Mother of Compassion,
               Sisters of Providence Motherhouse,
               Kingston, Ontario

Printed in Canada.

McNorgan, David, 1954-
Preparing the environment for worship

(Preparing for liturgy)

Includes bibliographical references.

ISBN 2-89088-797-9

1. Catholic Church–Liturgical objects. 2. Liturgy and architecture. I. Title. II. Series.

BX1970.3.M34 1997   246   C97-900969-3

Contents

Introduction

We human beings are not angels. Our praise of God has flesh and bones, and when we pray at liturgy, we do so with our entire bodies. Every sensate experience, all that we see, taste, touch, smell, and hear is not merely inspiration for some more authentic interior kind of prayer. Rather, in the very acts of listening, eating, drinking, walking, immersing, anointing and so on, we pray, celebrating and deepening our relationship with God and each other in the body of Christ.

The art of preparing the environment for liturgy, therefore, is a ministry to prayer and a service to the human body. Persons who wish to take on this labour of love are privileged indeed as they open other persons to God's mysteries through the beauty of material creation. What follows in this book are some reflections and suggestions to help you in your work.

CHAPTER 1

The Work of the Environment

Form Follows Function

"Form follows function" is the architect's adage. When preparing the environment, liturgy planners first consider what ritual actions worshippers will perform. For example, gathering is our first liturgical act. The arrangement of seating must allow us to experience the presence of other persons and enable our common actions. The primary function that determines what form we give to any element in the environment is the full, active participation of the faithful in the liturgy.

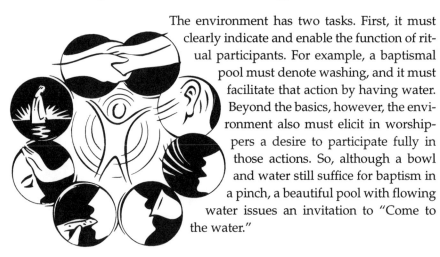

The environment has two tasks. First, it must clearly indicate and enable the function of ritual participants. For example, a baptismal pool must denote washing, and it must facilitate that action by having water. Beyond the basics, however, the environment also must elicit in worshippers a desire to participate fully in those actions. So, although a bowl and water still suffice for baptism in a pinch, a beautiful pool with flowing water issues an invitation to "Come to the water."

Environment and ritual interaction

The environment is not simply "out there." We are part of it when we use symbols in the performance of ritual actions. We hear words, drink wine, eat bread, anoint with oil, sing music, immerse in water, and so on. The liturgical environment is, by nature, interactive. Nothing in the environment is static.

Because of this interactive quality, the assembly itself is the environment's first and most important element. Members of the assembly should come with bodies prepared for the work of prayer. This work is to sing, breathe, listen, stand, sit, kneel, eat, drink, touch, smell, taste, feel and move. We prepare all other elements of the environment, such as bread, wine, vessels, font, furnishings, oil, water, and so on in ways that the assembly might do its work with these symbols, that the assembly might exercise its ministry of full, conscious, active participation in the liturgy.

Ritual Has a Tradition

Our rituals, though they evolve, have been handed down to us by previous generations. The liturgical environment, therefore, must submit itself to the constraints of genuine tradition. Persons who prepare the environment should be familiar with the elements that mark Roman Catholic rituals such as particular symbols and gestures, formal texts, the ordering of ministries, and the cycle of liturgical seasons.

However, the environment is part of a living tradition, not dead custom. Our liturgical actions must also be relevant enough to the contemporary community that we can bring to life the ways of praying that our forebears passed on. To be creative is not to invent new rituals. Creativity is preparing the riches of our tradition in such a way that the community celebrating today may experience the liturgy's symbols and gestures revealing God-with-us now in this time and place.

Ritual Is Performative

Language is performative, that is, when we use words something happens. Words not only communicate information; they also shape attitudes and relationships. The exchange of marriage vows unites two persons legally, morally and spiritually. "OK" enacts an agreement. Saying "I'm sorry" effects reconciliation. "I apologize" works for political or social mistakes, but lacks sufficient depth for personal relationships. Words perform. They do what they say. Further, the nuances of the voice and facial expressions carry the meaning of the words. Sometimes these subtle non-verbal elements will add weight to words. At other times, the non-verbal nuances suggest we can take the verbal communication with a grain of salt.

Like words, ritual actions also effect relationships and attitudes. A handshake, for example, is a social ritual. With it we can welcome a stranger or effect a contractual agreement. A firm grip or a limp extension of the hand will nuance the ritual. Thus, the kind of handshake exchanged shapes the quality of interaction between persons. It enacts an attitude of trust or distrust, and defines one's willingness to enter into a relationship with another. Social rituals, whether gestures, seating arrangements at dinners or salutations, are performative. They make relationships happen. Ritual actions do what they "say," and the context and style of their performance communicates many nuanced levels of meaning.

The Environment Is Performative

The liturgical environment also does what it says. Every object, furnishing, colour, smell, taste, sound and gesture has a performative character. They shape relationships and fashion in participants a way of being with one another in prayer.

We human beings embody prayer with our senses. At evening prayer, for example, as we smell incense and watch its swirling clouds rise heavenward, the ritual enacts our relationship with God. Our sensate experience of fragrant smoke is not mere inspiration for prayer "in our hearts," as if disembodied prayer would be more authentic. Rather, the ritual action—in the case of evening prayer the experience of music, words, smoke, censer, fire, darkness, bowing, sitting, standing—is our prayer. Our ritual interaction with these elements, our common attentiveness and participation, these acts form us into a people in relationship with God. Over time the repeated performance of these ritual actions gradually shapes lives marked by sacrifice and thanksgiving.

Ritual Is Repetitive

Rituals are performative because they are repetitive. Ritual words and gestures work because we know what to expect. Year after year we sing "Happy Birthday." Each day we kiss goodbye, hello, and goodnight. When we meet a friend we embrace. If we had to re-invent such gestures every time we used them we would never be able to establish social relationships.

Knowing what to expect is not boring. The familiarity that comes with repetition lets us go deeper each time we return to liturgy. Ritual familiarity is much like living with a person for years. You come to know and anticipate each other's ways, without taking the other for granted, or becoming weary of the other. Spiritual drowsiness comes from inattentiveness, not from familiarity and repetition. As another writer once said, if the routine of ritual seems boring, it is because you haven't done it long enough.

Elements of the liturgical environment, if they are to have the power to shape relationships of prayer, must be repetitive. We must be able to return to them like a familiar home, able to contemplate, savour, and plumb their depths day by day, week by week. For example, accessible settings for psalms let their words seep into our souls. Well-known acclamations enable us to acclaim. The familiarity of bringing ourselves before the ambo, lectionary and reader each week fashions us into hearers of God's word. Preparers of the liturgical environment must work to build not only a house, but a home for the church.

Sensate symbols

Preparing the environment for liturgy is a task of anticipating and making ready every tactile, visual, oral, olfactory, kinesthetic, and gustatory experience the worshipping assembly will have. Good preparation ensures the full expression of symbols, and enables our full, conscious, active participation in the ritual.

Liturgy's environment is more than the arrangement of flowers and furnishings. It is everything we see, hear, smell, taste, touch, or sense in any way with our bodies. The environment is:

Aural: everything we hear—music: vocal, instrumental, choral, a cappella; voices: pace, cadence, inflection, timbre;

Gustatory: everything we taste—bread, wine;

Olfactory: everything we smell—incense, beeswax, flowers, bread and wine, wood;

Kinesthetic: our physical movements—our body awareness of movement and proximity to other elements of physical environment; acts such as processing, marking self with the sign of the cross, handshakes and embraces at the peace, standing, sitting, kneeling, genuflecting, eating, drinking;

Tactile: everything we touch—baptismal water, bread and wine, hymnals, ritual books, other persons, the cup, wine, bread;

Visual: everything we see—walkways, landscape, doors, vestibules, seats, baptismal pool and water, ambo, altar table, architectural structures and shapes, other persons, light, colours, textures.

Most liturgical symbols are a mix of many sensate experiences, that is, we see, hear, taste, touch, move and smell all at once. For example, we hear the psalm, its text, melody, and accompaniment. We see the cantor; we feel a book in our hands; we hear and feel the resonance of our own singing in our bodies, the movement of air in our diaphragms; we hear and feel the nearness of someone next to us who is also singing. All of these sensate experiences make up our experience of praying the psalm at liturgy. Preparing the environment for this particular moment of prayer requires that we provide a good sound system, quality music and instruments, a trained cantor and attractive books or programs. Members of the assembly prepare to pray the psalm by sitting, breathing and being attentive.

Symbols Are Real

The common remark that some gesture or object is "only a symbol," implying that it is less than authentic, does a great disservice to a good understanding of liturgical symbols. Symbols, in fact, can carry more truth than do literal statements. They have a power to convey the nuances and inexhaustible meaning of human relationships in a way that logic and reason cannot.

Think of reality as what grows in us like the tissue of life. What is real does not drop out of the sky, but it is found in the accumulated layers of meaning developed through a lifetime of being attentive to the world around us, of growing in understanding and responsibility, and living out relationships of self-giving love. Symbols, such as gestures of affection, a birthday cake, the home we live in, music, art, the wonder of a sunset, the sound of wind—all of these non-verbal expressions continually draw us deeper into relationships with ourselves, others and God.

Symbols are ritual's "language." Compared to a piece of music, symbols are like the notes, and the ritual act is the performance of the score. Symbols are not static; they convey their meaning when we perform actions with them. Persons who prepare liturgy's symbols, therefore, must prepare them for full expression. Bread, for example, must appear and taste as natural food that persons might eat. The table is prepared for gathering, the word for hearing, and so on. Nothing in liturgy is prepared for mere display.

When symbols are used for display and not full participation, they become minimal and petrified. If the assembly were only allowed to listen to a professional choir or soloists, and could never sing its liturgical song, that symbol of music would become petrified and lifeless. If the eucharistic bread were reduced to a thin tasteless wafer, or if the cup was not offered to everyone, then the banquet's minimal expression as food and drink would lessen our full participation in the mysteries we celebrate.

In Summary

1. Preparing the environment is a ministry of prayer and a service to the human body.

2. The environment serves the ritual. Know the shape and elements of whatever rite you are celebrating.

3. The liturgical environment is everything we see, hear, smell, taste, touch or sense in any way with our bodies.

4. Preparing the environment aims to recover the full expression of liturgy's symbols and the assembly's full participation in liturgy's symbolic actions.

Discussion Questions

1. With your liturgy committee, make a list of all aural, visual, gustatory, olfactory, tactile, kinesthetic elements in your liturgical environment.

2. Does your liturgical community fully express these symbols in your worship? Do any suffer from minimalism and petrification?

3. Which ones can you begin to renew?

CHAPTER 2

Environment and Ritual

The environment serves the shape of liturgy. Preparing the environment, therefore, is much more than arranging flowers and hanging banners. It is a work of arranging objects, furnishings, movements, sights, sounds, colours, tastes, aromas and textures in such a way that persons can gather for prayer, hear and contemplate God's word in scriptures, and participate fully in whatever ritual action is part of the rite.

Assembly Required

Our arrangement of the environment should suggest it needs people to complete it. The environment is not a display, but a space for action. The assembly's full, active participation is the crux of ritual action. Particular ministers never perform ritual on behalf of others. The assembly is always the active minister of prayer, and particular ministers are themselves members of the assembly.

The environment must shape in all worshippers an attitude that their participation is essential to the liturgy. In practice this means that no focal point looks like a stage, and no minister acts as a solo performer. All decoration and art supportively participates in the ritual actions at hand.

Liturgy's First Symbol

Arriving at church, we see friends, acquaintances and strangers. We exchange gestures of greeting, catch up on the week's happenings. Ministers hand out programs with the order of service and assist persons with the practicalities of assembling such as getting up a step, using a lift device, or opening a door. The hospitality these ministers show is itself an invitation to participate fully in the liturgy.

The many faces and bodies that begin to fill the worship space become the environment. Just as we human beings do not know ourselves *outside* of our bodies, on this side of heaven we know ourselves as members of the body of Christ only *in* our flesh and blood human existence. The assembly of people is liturgy's first symbol and the environment must first shape a disparate group of people into an assembly. In the very physical nature of our relationships and ritual actions we become Christ's presence in the world.

Accessibility

If our worshipping community is to include all persons in the body of Christ, the liturgical environment must be physically accessible.

For persons who are unable to climb stairs, the building requires a grade level entry, ramp, or lift device. Where there is a raised sanctuary, we also need a ramp inside the church leading up to the ambo or altar table. Further, if the choir loft and parish hall are on other levels, they, too, should be accessible that persons might participate fully in the liturgical and social life of their community.

If you remove some seats in the nave to create a larger seating area for persons in wheelchairs, these accessible spaces need not always be in the front row. Consider the need for persons in wheelchairs to see, hear and participate in liturgical actions, but also their desire to feel integrated into the assembly, not set apart from it.

Aural Accessibility

People need to hear the sounds of liturgy if they are to participate fully in its aural prayer. A worshipping community should expect to spend several thousand dollars on an excellent sound system for the benefit of everyone. The system must also have FM receiver units for persons who are hearing-impaired. Hearing devices do not provide 100 per cent comprehension of sounds, so they must be augmented. You can also reserve seats for hearing-impaired persons so they can lip read when particular ministers are speaking or singing. Further, texts of readings and prayers should be provided for persons who cannot hear everything that is spoken. For persons who communicate in American Sign Language (ASL), the church has the responsibility to provide interpreters.

Beauty Awakens the Body

The gathering of persons for liturgy awakens our bodiliness, that we might become what we celebrate. Such an awakening requires that everything we see, hear, smell, and touch at liturgy should be beautiful to the senses. Beauty has the power to stir body, mind, and soul to wakeful attentiveness.

Beauty is a quality of design. In his delightful book *Everybody Steals From God: Communication as Worship*, Edward Fischer describes four characteristics that apply to all designs, whether in nature, art, mathematics, architecture, ritual, or whatever. Virtually everywhere you look you discover design and its elements of unity, variety, balance and harmony.

Unity is that idea of a design that holds it all together. In a musical piece, for example, without the unity of a motif or theme we would merely have a chaotic collection of notes. Liturgy's unity is in the paschal mystery, the source and goal of all we are and do. The ritual motif that unifies the liturgical act is the full, active participation of the assembly, a theme that imbues every element of the environment. Without these two unifying themes, the paschal mystery and the full active participation of the faithful, our words, symbols and gestures would be disconnected from prayer and Christian discipleship. We would lapse into either magic or mindless cultism.

Variety keeps a design from getting dull. Liturgy's rhythm of speech and song, movement and stillness, and its arousal of all the human senses are not mere ploys for maintaining interest. Rather the rhythm and the sensory quality of liturgy reflect the very designs we find in nature itself, rhythms of time and seasons in a universe bursting in myriad explosions of sound, sight, taste, smell and touch. Liturgy's rhythms and sensate qualities invite us to be attentive, to wonder, and to celebrate the variety of life itself.

Variety also occurs in the artistic creation of all elements in the liturgical environment. Works crafted by artisans and musicians are far more interesting and engaging than those that are commercially produced. A craftsperson will follow the elements of good design, but the touch of the unexpected that emerges from the potter's wheel, or the spirit of the moment that inspires a musician's performance—these qualities can never be reproduced in bulk. This authenticity of craft, which is an element of beauty, elicits appreciation and awe. It is the reason we have live musicians at liturgy and not taped music, and why we should commission artists and craftspersons to create furnishings, vestments, and other liturgical objects for our prayer.

Balance is essential to the design and healthy function of ecological systems. Similarly, it is a quality of a good liturgical environment. In a balanced liturgical space every element interacts with and depends on others. For example, seating shapes a habitat where the assembly can perform its ministry of full, active participation. However, if an ornate sanctuary visually overwhelms the seating, the resulting imbalance can inhibit the assembly and eventually render us lifeless. Confined to pews that feel passive and secondary, if we try to sing or act together, a sense of vertigo will throw us back to the stability of private piety. The problem of individualism at liturgy is as much one of imbalance in the environment as it is one of apathy or ill will.

Harmony has to do with things working together. An artist composes a dance or poem or painting so that nothing can rightly be added or taken away. Similarly, harmony in the liturgical environment shows when every gesture, word and symbol impregnates our lives with meaning. Nothing in the liturgical environment is superfluous, or added merely to spice things up. For example, if a banner appears, it has some supportive connection to the ritual action that occurs around it. Or when we make music, we don't embellish the liturgy, we embody it, giving flesh and bones to our prayer.

The more the liturgical environment can embody the characteristics of good design, the more beautiful our prayer will be. And the more beautiful the prayer, the more we open in wonder, awe and gratitude before the mystery of God among us.

In Summary

1. The environment must actively engage all the senses. While it must be beautiful to look at, it is not primarily for visual display.

2. The assembly is liturgy's first symbol. Human persons interact with liturgy's symbols and space.

3. Assembly required: Everything in the environment should invite the assembly's full active participation.

4. Beauty in the worship space stirs us to attentiveness. Beauty comes from unity, variety, balance and harmony in design.

5. Accessibility is essential for persons who are hearing-impaired or have difficulty climbing steps. The body of Christ is physically inclusive.

Discussion Questions

1. Get a panoramic view of your worship space. How does this environment need people to complete it?

2. Do focal points and symbols enable and invite the ritual actions that the assembly must perform?

3. Observe the entire space and individual furnishings and objects. Are they beautiful? How do they embody the four elements of design?

4. Consider your space from the perspective of accessibility. What are the major difficulties for people with different kinds of disabilities? How can your community work to overcome them?

CHAPTER 3

Transitional Space

When we move from home to liturgy, we need a transitional space because ritual's actions, symbols, and environment engage our bodies and minds with an almost exaggerated intensity that we could not endure in our daily routines. Ordinary experiences are no less holy than the actions we perform at church. But the latter are not daily fare, so we need to cross over from the commonplace to a ritual way of being.

Even before the first utterance of liturgical texts, every element of the environment shapes our transition and affects the quality of prayer that follows. The experiences of moving from home to car, from parking lot to front door, from vestibule to seat—these sights, sounds, smells, movements and feelings begin to fashion attitudes and relationships of prayer.

Hospitality

Where the environment has a quality of hospitality there will be community. Hospitality is more than being greeted by a friendly face, although it is at least that much. Hospitality evokes a sense of belonging to activities and to the spaces in which they occur. Participants feel welcome when hymn books or worship aids are readily available, when other voices make an effort at communal singing, when music is beautifully performed, when a reader proclaims the scriptures expressively, or when another person offers a sincere gesture of Christ's peace. Such hospitality communicates to a ritual participant: "this moment, every gesture and symbol belong to you; this gathering place, this ritual is your home; you are no stranger here."

Liturgical hospitality invites our full, active participation in the ritual experience. It is a characteristic of the assembly, a quality of the environment, and an attribute in those who perform particular ministries. It is the ease and willingness with which persons interact; it is the familiarity of worshippers with their ritual; it is the evocative power of every word, object and gesture, everything that liturgy offers to taste, touch, smell, see and hear. Such is the hospitality that makes the litur-gy and its environment an experi-ence of being at home, at prayer, with God's people.

All persons at worship are responsible for this quality in the liturgy. Persons who prepare the envi-ronment, choreograph gestures, rehearse readings, practice music, as well as members of the assembly who exhibit an openness and willingness to participate fully—all these are ministers of hospitality. Persons who facilitate the transition of worshippers through the vestibule are more properly called greeters. To assign them the weight of hospitality is too much of a burden for any single ministry.

Pathways

Picture in your mind a pathway from the parking lot winding its way through shrubs, flowers and trees. This walk from asphalt to doorway can be more than a sidewalk. It is the body's and heart's preparation for liturgy. On a well-designed path worshippers can take time to smell the blossoms and flowers, nature's fragrant offering to the Lord of creation. Benches will offer a respite, a chance to slow down and catch our spiritual breath. The sights, smells and sounds we experience walking this path each week awaken our senses to our relationship with the Creator and with each other. We pray as we walk.

Sounds

Bells peal, toll, chime. Their sound can celebrate a marriage, announce a death, or tell the town what time it is. Bells have a unique power to gather the dispersed from afar. Their ringing does not call us in from the fields these days, but their reverberation through the outdoor air still elicits our attentiveness and directs us to a common focus.

Other sounds also shape this transitional space. They are the welcoming timbre of human voices—young, old, stranger, friend, women and men. These sounds embody our diversity and hospitality.

Outdoor Signs

There is an ugly creature creeping onto the lawns of many churches. It is the marquee, that public signboard with fluorescent memos for the entire neighbourhood. Big plastic block letters convey messages like HAVE A GOOD DAY. Even religious exhortations, such as "Jesus Loves You" or "Alleluia," lack depth in this cold, two-dimensional medium. Such a mode of evangelization trivializes our faith. The strongest signs of welcome and witness are the beauty of architecture, trees, walkways, and especially the gathering of people for worship.

The Threshold

For persons who want to become followers of Jesus there is a threshold to cross, a passing over from death to life. Adults mark this passover with a lengthy period of formation and rites of initiation. After our initial crossing, we pass through death again and again when we gather for eucharist, the weekly renewal and celebration of our baptismal life. And we cross the threshold a final time when fellow sojourners gather for our rites of Christian burial.

Many elements of the environment, especially at the church entrance, embody this threshold character of Christian spirituality. As persons enter the church, they experience first the door, vestibule, and baptismal pool as signs of our passage through death to life.

Doors

Some communities might be happy just to have a door to keep the cold out and the heat in, no matter how fancy. True, form follows function, but the door has more than a practical purpose. It is a barrier to inclement weather, but the doorway also becomes a portal to the paschal mystery. Consider the effects of different materials and designs on our experience of feeling drawn into this mystery.

Glass, wood, steel, vinyl, hinged, revolving, sliding—these materials and designs convey different attitudes. Some are suitable for homes, some for grocery stores. For churches, glass doors through which you can see what is happening on the other side might reveal too much too easily, lacking a threshold character. Large steel doors could be too imposing, sliding doors too expedient. The warmth of wood's grain and colour might best elicit in persons who approach the threshold a desire to enter the mystery. Whatever material and design, the doors must work in harmony with other elements in the entry way to draw us into Christ's life, death, and resurrection and anticipate the work of liturgical prayer.

A Common Entrance

Church entrances express the inclusive and communal character of our Christian passover. Where the doorway is not at grade level, steps reach out onto the sidewalk like a mother's arms and gather God's children. The doors are larger than the front door of a private home. Their size alone invites many people to come in. When we enter through a common doorway we begin our act of gathering as an assembly. A multitude of entrances, on the other hand, would scatter worshippers' attention. Where several entrances from the outside are required, they can at least lead to a common focus in the vestibule, such as the baptismal pool, then direct persons to a single doorway into the body of the church. An assembly hall must have several *exits* for fire regulations, but these doors need not be used as entrances. Our entry into the church is our first ritual act, and a single entrance makes that movement a common act of gathering.

The Vestibule

Imagine the foyer of your own home. When you are preparing for some special occasion, what attitudes and relationships do you want the vestibule to convey to guests as they come through the door? The foyer provides an hospitable transition into the main living space of your home. Similarly, worshippers need a well-prepared vestibule to make their transition to a ritual way of acting. Is there a place to hang coats? Once you've celebrated liturgy with your coat off, you'll never go back! Do signs point to washrooms and diaper-changing facilities? Are they subtle, yet clearly visible? After taking care of basic creature comforts, consider the human need for beauty. Keep shovels, brooms, ice salt, and extra chairs out of sight, but readily available. The church vestibule has to function, but it doesn't have to resemble the family mud room.

The job of maintaining the vestibule and outside approach ways is so important that it should be given to one person on the liturgy committee. This person must be good at balancing the functional and the aesthetic elements in a space. Each season, feast or celebration requires different accents. Flowers, colourful ribbons, seasonal art, banners, crèches, food collection baskets, photographs of parishioners and parish ministers, Development and Peace tables, cultural holiday symbols such as cornucopias and Christmas trees—these tone-setting decorations can best connect our liturgical prayer with our daily living when we set them in the transitional space of the vestibule, not in the sanctuary. The sanctuary has different, more important, focal points.

In Summary

1. Hospitality is found in the familiarity and evocative power of every element in the environment.

2. Entrances are the thresholds that we cross to become followers of Christ.

3. The design of pathways, sounds, doors and the vestibule elicits in those who approach a desire to enter. Imbued with beauty, the transitional space can carry the weight of mystery, suggesting that one who makes this pilgrimage will journey into a realm where "eye has not seen and ear has not heard what God has ready."

Discussion Questions

1. Make slides of your church's environment, both exterior and interior and use them regularly at liturgy committee meetings for discussion.

2. Identify what people experience when they approach and first enter the worship space. Is the space accessible for all? How does the entry way convey or inhibit hospitality?

CHAPTER 4

The Baptismal Environment

The most striking object in the entry way, if you choose to locate it there, is the baptismal pool. What better way to begin every liturgy than to dip your hand in the flowing waters of baptism and mark yourself with the sign of Jesus' passage to life through death!

We make our passover with Christ through our full participation in the rites of Christian initiation and their symbols of assembly, font, water, oil, fire, and white garment. Preparing the baptismal area is a matter of expressing these symbols fully and harmoniously.

For the Assembly

Many new constructions and renovations provide an area at the church entrance for a baptismal pool, either in the vestibule or just inside the nave. This location works well for several reasons. First, it signifies baptism as a rite of initiation into the liturgical community. Second, it allows and invites persons to use baptismal water at the beginning of other liturgies as a sign of our participation in the life of Christ. Wedding and funeral processions pass by these waters of baptism. It is a most appropriate symbol for a Christian bride and groom to use at the beginning of their sojourn into the life, death, and resurrection of Christ, or for friends and family to sign the coffin carrying the body of their loved one who now ends the earthly journey.

Whether at the entrance or elsewhere in the midst of the assembly, the area for baptism must allow and encourage the full participation of the faithful, especially at the Easter Vigil.

Full Expression of Water

Some baptismal fonts are pools designed for full immersion, about knee deep with water. They are large enough to contain at least the church's minister and the person being baptized. For baptism the catechumen kneels, and the minister lowers his or her head forward and under the water three times while reciting the baptismal formula. Other pools have two levels. On the upper level is a large concave vessel, into which water is pumped. It should be large enough to accommodate an infant for immersion. Water flows from this upper bowl to a large pool below, and recirculates to the upper level. The lower level of the pool is large enough to stand in, and the minister baptizes by pouring generous amounts of water over the standing or kneeling catechumen.

To construct and maintain a full or partial immersion font requires commitment from persons who prepare the liturgy. From the church's ministers of baptism it demands a willingness to fully express baptism's symbols. If a large pool is something new, the minister should have a "wet" run with members of the liturgy committee to get a feel for expressing fully the gestures and symbols of initiation, and identify practical considerations such as water temperature, slippery floors, appropriate clothing, and so on.

Flowers and foliage in the baptismal area communicate new life. Plants should serve the font, not overwhelm it. You can change them seasonally to mark the rhythms of the liturgical year. One parish drained its full immersion font and removed greenery during Lent. For persons accustomed to blessing themselves with its water each Sunday, the absence was a stark reminder of Lent's austere tone. The resurgence of living water at the Easter Vigil made for a joyful celebration of Christ's victory over death.

The Ambry

The ambry is a cabinet or recess in the church wall for holding sacred vessels of oil. This cabinet for the holy oils is located near the font, not only for convenience, but to show oil as a primary symbol of initiation. A glass front on the cabinet displays the holy oils beautifully in their containers. These might be blown glass bottles, each a different colour. The colours give variety and can evoke feelings associated with healing, life in God's Spirit, and walking the journey of faith. Worshippers who pass by the ambry each Sunday see the rich texture of the oils and the beauty of the bottles and cabinet. These symbols remind them of their own baptismal journey, and their own need for the healing balm of Christ.

The Easter Candle

This candle is the première source of ritual fire, a symbol of Christ's presence as light in the darkness. Its stand should be strong and visible. The candle is beautiful in its simplicity. It should always stand erect. Encourage parents or godparents to light their children's baptismal candle from the paschal flame. At eucharistic liturgies where this candle burns, use a taper to take its flame to candles near the altar table at the preparation of gifts. Have a family member carry it in the funeral mass procession for their loved one. Process reverently with the paschal candle at the Easter vigil and evening prayer, graciously offering it to the faithful who hold out their tapers, their very selves to receive the light of Christ.

The White Garment

To signify more fully the mystery of our being clothed in Christ, prepare substantial white garments for infants and adults. The garment should resemble a robe, not a stole, which is a symbol of ordained ministry. When a baptism takes place, these white garments might be held by assistants or draped on a stand nearby, visible to all. After persons are clothed at baptism, allow them to keep the robe. It is a powerful reminder of this ritual act of putting on Christ. When a person dies, we might include their baptismal garment in the liturgical environment at the funeral home or church. Some persons might wish to be buried in their baptismal robe.

In Summary

1. The baptismal area requires preparing a space for the full expression of the symbols of assembly, pool, water, oil, fire, and the white robe.

2. Prepare a space for gathering, plentiful water, an ambry with beautiful vessels for oil, a prominent Easter Candle, and a substantial white garment for the newly baptized.

Discussion Questions

1. With your liturgy committee, remember significant experiences with water, whether pleasurable or terrifying. Awaken yourselves to the power of water in human life, then discuss the value of a fuller expression of water in the ritual of baptism.

2. After a person is baptized and anointed in your community, does the minister quickly remove water and oil with a towel, or do they let the newly baptized linger in the sensate experience of those symbols?

3. How might your ritual environment and actions more fully express the symbols of fire and the white baptismal robe in baptism?

4. Do persons being baptized, their godparents, and families feel that they are active participants in the rite? Or do they feel like passive recipients of the minister's actions? How do our actions with baptismal symbols enable participation or engender passivity?

CHAPTER 5

Dealing with Space

For the environment to enable common prayer, the relationship between the assembly's seating and the focal points of liturgical actions must possess elements of good design. These elements are unity, variety, balance and harmony, qualities that give beauty to design. These four elements work together to create a space in which no object or minister dominates the ritual experience.

Unity

Unity in the environment fashions common unity in the assembly. A good arrangement of chairs enables persons to see each other, to feel they are acting together, and to participate fully around the various focal points of the liturgical action.

The different focal points, namely the presider's chair, ambo and altar table, are placed so as to shift our attention at different moments in the liturgy. To clump them together in one place fails to engage participants in the shift of focus from gathering, to word, to eucharist.

Balance

Balance gives each element in the environment its due. For example, the presider's chair when set in close proximity to the assembly, conveying clearly that minister's role to preside over, not dominate, the ritual. However, if a huge altar eclipses a puny lectern, the resulting imbalance suggests the word is less important than the eucharist, and enfeebles the assembly's full participation in both parts of the liturgy.

Harmony

Harmony in the environment shows when furnishings, objects and spaces serve each other according to the nature of liturgy. For example, simple arrangements of green plants can bring life to a cavernous space. However, don't let huge floral displays overwhelm more important focal points. Harmony in the environment brings oneness to our ritual actions when worshippers interact with one another and the symbols with which they pray.

The Problem of Sanctuaries

Roman Catholic liturgy requires a "house for the church," a place in which believers may gather and take active roles in the praise of God. Affirming the presence of Christ in all believers does not turn us into an amorphous mass. Liturgy does require focal points, such as altar table, ambo, presider's chair, and music area, and different ministries such as presider, cantor, musicians, eucharistic ministers, lector, and deacon. However, that differentiation of focal points and ministries does not require that we rigidly separate the assembly from its particular ministers, and set focal points for ritual actions on a stage-like platform built across one narrow end of a long rectangular room.

The problem of a raised stage facing rows of benches is that persons in the pews are implicitly consigned to the role of spectator. The best presiding, music, reading and decorations will never overcome the individualism and isolation that such an environment perpetuates. Good liturgy will help us tolerate bad seating, but a poor environment will keep us from praying as fully as we want to.

For this reason many worshipping communities renovate their liturgical space. When we can't live in our home as we want to, because of a growing family or changing life situations, then we either move out, rebuild or renovate. Similarly, in the house of the church, when we can no longer pray as we want to, it is time to change things around.

Changing Rectangular Spaces

Fan-shaped semi-circular seating in newer church constructions attempts to overcome the problem of the long rectangular space. However, those new churches usually retain a stage-like sanctuary that will continue to suggest the ministers "up front" are acting on behalf of the people "out there." People in the pews have greater peripheral vision of other worshippers, but can easily continue to feel relegated to spectator status.

In a long rectangular church, some communities have turned the entire space sideways, whereby the length becomes the width. Sometimes this design retains a sanctuary, but it feels less remote or dominating. Seats wrap around the focal points in a horse-shoe shape.

Other sideways renovations have eliminated the familiar sanctuary platform altogether. Instead the space has distinct focal points placed separately throughout the assembly. In this scenario, the ambo, altar table, and chair are set on three separate, and much smaller, raised platforms. The location and the height make the actions at those focal points visible and audible. Yet, the intermingling of focal points with the assembly's seating conveys strongly that this liturgy is the action of the entire people of God. The apse, which formerly contained the sanctuary, is now used for the music ministry or, perhaps, as the baptismal area.

Other renovated narrow spaces arrange the seating choir-style, rows of seats on two sides facing in towards a long aisle. At one end of this axis is the ambo. Slightly in from the other end, or in the centre of the axis is the altar table. The presider's chair is at the end opposite the ambo. Again, the music area might be in the apse.

Seating

Benches or chairs in the environment must let members of the assembly fully participate according to their role. Seating has not always been a part of Christian worship spaces. Nevertheless, it is difficult to imagine gathering people for our present-day order of service without providing a place to sit.

Chairs offer more flexibility than benches. Don't create confusion by rearranging the furniture too often. Nevertheless, we might welcome the freedom to remove some chairs for a smaller assembly, or turn some towards the font for baptism, or create a different seating pattern for various seasons or celebrations.

We're Stuck with What We Have!

Perhaps you have little choice but to continue worshipping in a long rectangular space. If a major renovation is not possible for your community at this time, here are some suggestions to keep you going.

- Get a good sound system. Ensure voices and music are audible and warm, not cold or distant. If people can hear, and if they hear themselves making beautiful sounds, they will feel they are active participants in what is going on.

- Create a sense of unity in the sanctuary and nave with balanced lighting. Talk with a lighting consultant who understands liturgy. The use of bright and warm spotlights in the sanctuary contrasted with dim or fluorescent lights in the nave will cast a shadow of passivity or coldness on the assembly.

- If you have to replace the carpet in the sanctuary, use the same floor coverings in both the nave and sanctuary. The sanctuary itself is not a focal point, so there is no reason to differentiate its floor covering.

- Avoid using the sanctuary as a display centre for decorations. Place seasonal art, banners, flowers, and the like throughout the whole church. Surround the assembly in beauty to unify it in prayer.

- Unclutter the sanctuary. Remove extra chairs. All you need is one for the presider. Altar servers, lectors and communion ministers can sit elsewhere.

- Move the tabernacle out of the sanctuary to a separate chapel or a transept.

- When ministers, such as the lector, enter the sanctuary, do not have them bow to the presider or to any object. A bow or genuflection upon entering and leaving the church will suffice. Extra gestures of reverence during the liturgy only accentuate the separation of the assembly from the sanctuary and the presider. Persons who minister from the sanctuary space should do so with confidence and grace.

In Summary

1. The assembly's seating must allow persons to participate around the focal points of altar, ambo, presider's chair, and music area.

2. The common separation of sanctuary and nave is an obstacle to overcome.

3. Avoid any arrangement of furnishings, any decoration or actions that treat the assembly like spectators or make particular ministers look like entertainers.

Discussion Questions

1. Consider balance in the aural environment. How do sounds of music and the presider's voice facilitate full participation at liturgy? Do these sounds in any way dominate or cause imbalance in the worship experience?

2. In nature, where do you find beauty in simplicity? Discuss ways to unclutter your sanctuary.

3. Have your committee experience liturgy in differently designed spaces. Share and discuss feelings each environment elicits. What values and relationships do you want your space to communicate?

CHAPTER 6

Focal Points

The Presider's Chair

The presider participates in the liturgy as a member of the worshipping assembly who has a particular ministry of leadership. To signify the unity of presider and assembly the presider's chair should balance and harmonize with the assembly's seating. The chair can be distinctive, yet share similar materials, colour, and style with the assembly's chairs or benches. Balance also requires that its location clearly convey that the presider is part of the assembly. Depending on the size of the worship space, the chair might be set on a raised platform to ensure the presider's gestures are visible and words audible. Nevertheless, the assembly must experience its presider, not as distant or aloof, but as an active, mutual participant.

Except for the eucharistic prayer, all presidential prayers are said from the presider's chair. The visual connection of the presider and chair provides a unifying symbol for common prayer. If the presider stands at the altar to lead the introductory rite, he mistakenly focuses worshippers on the liturgy of eucharist before it is time. Similarly, the presider recites the communion prayer from the chair, not the altar, because table sharing is finished and we are making the transition back into daily living. Using the chair as a proper focal point for presiding respects the dynamic shape of liturgy and the changes of focus that occur throughout the ritual action.

Two Tables

The liturgy of the word and the liturgy of eucharist are so closely connected that they form a single act of worship (*CSL*, 56). The ambo, as table of the word, and the altar, as table of the eucharist, should be designed and arranged so that they clearly convey this unity of word and eucharist.

These two furnishings should be similar in style and materials. A table is naturally larger than a reading stand, but the altar table should not dwarf the ambo, thus suggesting the word is secondary. Nor do we need to set the altar table in the centre of the worship space, such that the ambo seems relegated to lesser status off to the side.

Balance and symmetry are not identical. Often we can achieve better balance in the environment by setting both the ambo and the altar off-centre. With the altar table and ambo in distinct but related positions, the assembly can shift its focus according to the part of the liturgy being celebrated.

The Ambo

The ambo is a privileged place for the word of God. It is good to get into the habit of calling it the ambo so as not to confuse it with a smaller lectern used for announcements and songleading. The ambo is reserved for the readings, responsorial psalm, and Easter proclamation. The homily and intercessions, because of their integral nature in the liturgy of the word, may also be delivered from the ambo, or from the presider's chair and a lectern respectively.

The qualities we look for in the proclamation of scriptures, namely clarity, simplicity and confidence, can also imbue the construction of the ambo. Clarity and simplicity in the ambo's design draw our attention to it. On this table of the word the book may rest with dignity; from it the reader is visible and audible. Any carvings on the ambo, or any fabric art or flowers nearby must be subtle, so as to not distract the assembly's attentiveness to the ambo and proclamation. Confidence, as a quality in the ambo, makes it strong. It is permanent, of significant size, and constructed of beautiful materials capable of bearing the dignity and mystery of God's word.

The Altar Table

The altar is the table of the Lord, a banquet table for all. Around this table the assembly may feel gathered under the leadership of a single presider. Its size is proportional to its function. It does not have to accommodate a phalanx of concelebrants, so a slightly rectangular, square, or round shape will better serve the assembly's need to gather than will an elongated structure.

To convey its unity with the ambo, the altar table should be constructed of similar materials and be harmonious in design. Wood, more than stone, seems a good material for conveying a sense of both altar and table. However, any natural material deemed worthy is suitable.

The only objects placed on the altar table during eucharist are bread and wine, and the sacramentary. Candles should not impede the view of the minister's actions or the faithful's perception that they assemble around the altar table. Large standing candles on each side of the altar table are too much like soldiers guarding against unwanted approach. Better to arrange them elsewhere nearby! Floral arrangements in this area should be simple enough to direct the assembly's attention to the altar table. Liturgy planners have a tendency to clutter the sanctuary with flowers, especially the altar table area. Remember, less is more.

At the fraction rite ministers who will assist with breaking the bread and pouring wine should approach the table respectfully and confidently. Hesitant body language conveys a reluctance to minister fully in the communion rite and will subtly discourage members of the assembly from fully taking their place at the table.

In Summary

1. Liturgy's table of the word and table of the eucharist must be designed and arranged with balance and harmony in mind.

2. These qualities enable the assembly to shift their focus at appropriate times, yet experience both word and eucharist as two parts of a single act of worship.

Discussion Questions

1. Are members of your community able to pray as they want to in the space that you have?

2. Where do people experience a sense of holiness in the liturgy and the environment?

3. Imagine what liturgy would feel like in a space without the familiar sanctuary. Discuss the possibilities your imaginings raise.

4. How can you overcome some of the obstacles to communal prayer posed by your present environment?

5. How might you arrange your altar table and ambo to invite equal attention to the liturgy of the word and the liturgy of the eucharist?

CHAPTER 7

The Things of the Liturgy

The Written Word

Various ministers require different books. The diversity of books reflects the diversity of ministries; no single minister uses all the books of liturgy. The assembly needs a hymnal. Lectors and deacons use a lectionary. The presider requires a sacramentary and other ritual books. All of these books should be beautifully bound to signify the importance of our rites. The word should never be read from a loose sheet of paper. Nor should copies of the readings be in the hands of the assembly or presider. Their role is to listen, not read.

If the assembly uses an order of service or occasional music, present the program attractively. Do not include texts for prayers and readings, only those parts to be sung or recited by the assembly. The presider uses a sacramentary as the prayer of the church. This book signifies the formal nature of liturgical prayer and this particular community's relationship with the larger church.

Book of the Gospels

The *Introduction to the Lectionary for Mass* encourages worshipping communities, especially larger ones, to use a Book of the Gospels. Without disrespecting the traditions of East and West, this writer considers the recovery of the ancient practice to be a dubious development for our present day.

Roman Catholics have regained a deep respect and love for scriptures, and for the Jewish people whose faith history the First Testament proclaims. We ritually separate the gospel from the rest of scripture by way of gestures, procession, acclamation, minister, greeting, responses and incense. One might argue that adding a second book merely supports what we do already. However, to further separate the gospels from other scriptures by using two books can perpetuate divisive attitudes, perhaps even anti-Semitic sentiments.

Persons perceive our present ritualization more as a division of clergy and laity than a sign of scripture's fulfillment in the story of Jesus Christ. The gospel appears as the priest's exclusive reading, accented as it is with candles, a sung acclamation, a procession, and ritual dialogue. This ritual embodiment, even though it is often weakly done, creates an imbalance with the ritualization of Christ's presence in the proclamation of the first two readings and the singing of the psalm.

If a community does use a Book of the Gospels, it has a duty to ritualize it well. The minister should be a deacon; the procession a walk through the midst of the assembly accompanied by praise-filled acclamation, and the homily a skilful oration that weaves together an awareness of God's Spirit moving through the experiences of all three scripture readings as well as the psalm, other liturgical texts and the lives of the people gathered. Persons who prepare liturgy should discern the community's prayer during the entire liturgy of the word, and not adopt a Book of the Gospels unthinkingly.

Vessels

The design and materials of containers we use for bread, wine, water, oil and incense must, of course, promote their liturgical function. Further, these vessels must elicit in the faithful a desire to participate in those functions.

Because vessels are made for the full, active participation of the assembly, these objects must be liturgically and culturally relevant. Ciboria, for example, are for bread, yet they often resemble large cups and denote drinking rather than eating. In a celebration where the meal character of eucharist receives little regard, and communion with both bread and wine is neglected, the shape of the ciboria may seem inconsequential. However, the material and shape of a liturgical plate or cup do fashion how we pray together. And when that way of praying is changing, so will the objects with which we pray.

New Wine, New Skins

On the altar table during the eucharistic prayer there is one plate for bread, ideally a single loaf. Also there is only one cup and, if more wine will be needed, a large flagon. Additional cups and plates remain on a side table until the fraction rite.

Common union in the body of Christ is the character of the communion rite. A single loaf of bread communicates that unity as do the design and materials of vessels used for the body and blood of Christ. No material can be singled out as more suitable than another. Gold, arguably, could seem inappropriate in a time when the victorious presence of Christ is less associated with triumph and wealth that it is with faithful service to persons who are powerless.

To embody unity, the cups should be of similar design. The cup used during the eucharistic prayer should also be offered to members of the assembly. No worshipper has his or her own private cup, not even the presider. For this reason we should discourage the gift of a chalice and paten to newly ordained presbyters, as if they are personal tools of the trade. Each assembly should decide the type of cups that best serves its worship; those cups should remain with the community.

If we use bread that tastes and appears as natural food we will have to rethink what containers best serve the ritual act of eating. Baskets are common for bread. Deep plates made from wood or clay might work well. Those preparing these liturgical objects should set aside preconceptions of what materials are holy. Then they can examine the works of various artisans to design what is suitable for their community.

It is true that the communion rite offers holy things for holy people. Some persons might deem anything less than silver or gold to be profane. However, no created material holds exclusive rights on sanctity. Or, rather, all creation holds such rights.

Persons preparing the environment need to contemplate designs and materials. They should look for liturgical vessels that are authentically and lovingly crafted, possessing a beauty that invites participation in the mystery they embody.

The Tabernacle

The tabernacle is a container for reserving communion for the sick. It also holds the consecrated eucharistic bread before which persons might pray outside of eucharist and further enter the mystery of Christ among us.

During the celebration of the eucharist the tabernacle has no function. Enough bread (hosts) should be consecrated for all participants at a particular celebration. Receiving bread consecrated at the eucharist we are celebrating signifies more completely our full participation in the mystery we celebrate (*General Instruction of the Roman Missal*, 56h). While preparing enough bread for each liturgy and consuming what is leftover does require some effort, where there is a will there is a way.

Because the tabernacle has no liturgical function it need not even be close to the worship space, but can be placed in a eucharistic chapel. When a separate chapel is not possible, the tabernacle should not compete with the altar table for visual attention. During eucharist no extra candles are lit near it. Nor should it be so adorned with flowers and spotlights that it distracts from liturgy's focal points. It can be set in a side transept, not front and centre. It can be on a pedestal or set into the wall, but not on a secondary altar. There is only one altar in the worship space around which we actively celebrate the Lord's Supper. A single candle constantly burning signifies our respect for the reserved eucharist.

Vesture

The physical presence of particular ministers has a symbolic value. Their bodies are part of the visual, aural and kinesthetic environment of worship. To this end, vesture can enhance their appearance and gestures. For example, in a large assembly, the gesture of extended arms and hands made by a presider could go unnoticed if he or she were wearing street clothes. The draping folds of an alb or chasuble, however, enable that gesture to become larger than the individual. The gesture, when made by a vested minister, can engage a large number of people in the gestures of the prayer. Conversely, in a small worship space such as a living room, such vesture could be too big for the environment.

Visual Art

How might we judge the value of works of art such as statues, banners, sculpture, mosaics, paintings, floral arrangements, seasonal decorations, and stations of the cross?

If a piece of art has no relation to the liturgical action that occurs around it, then it probably should be placed elsewhere. Some pieces, though not directly connected to a centre of action, can still support liturgy by creating and maintaining unity, balance and harmony in the liturgical space, while also adding a welcome element of variety.

Works of art support, but do not overwhelm, what they intend to enhance. For example, the altar table, ambo or baptismal area are more important than seasonal displays. If one looks towards any of these focal points and sees a proliferation of poinsettias or a grand banner dominating the visual scene, then these artistic displays are usurping, not serving, the liturgy.

Stations of the Cross

Stations of the cross hanging on the walls of the worship space work well because they enwrap the faithful in the passion, death and resurrection of Christ, our story at every liturgy. A large room also provides some distance for walking between stations during times of devotional prayer. However, in climes more favourable than those of most of Canada, placing the stations of the cross outdoors on a path that weaves its way throughout the church property could be one way of reclaiming this devotion as a pilgrim's meditation.

Banners

Colourful felt pieces on burlap marked an era in liturgical renewal. Many generous people spent hours cutting out letters and silhouettes to adorn the worship space. Making those banners gave them a sense of participating in the liturgy. Now, however, it is time to move forward, to leave behind our burlap message boards and be drawn into the beauty of fabric art. Budding artisans from the worshipping community can work with trained weavers and artists to fashion tapestries and hangings.

Think in images, colours and textures, not words. For example, a banner that adorns the baptismal area need not have words like "You are reborn in water and the spirit." The gestures of initiation convey that message, not only to the brain but to the whole person—body and mind, heart and soul.

Banners can support the baptismal ritual by evoking images such as water, life, death, fire and anointing. Choose colours and textures that might elicit feelings that accompany a Christian's passage to freedom, forgiveness and community. Beware of merely mimicking iconic clichés, such as a dove or tongues of fire. Spend time reflecting on the ritual moments that a particular piece of art will support. Get a feel for the rite and for the spiritual experience of those who participate in it.

For the baptismal area, imagine three tapestries, each woven in shades of brown, blue and red, allusions to earth, water and fire. Imagine these three long cloths hanging in different size semi-circular loops from the ceiling high above the pool, one end of each piece draping down toward the water. These lengths of cloth first draw our attention with their beauty, then focus us below to the pool and the actions taking place there. Without even saying the word "three," or using words to speak of the trinity, these three cloths work on the psyche as do symbolic numbers and colours, drawing us into relationship with God the Father, God the Son and God the Holy Spirit.

In Summary

1. The printed word in liturgical books and worship aids forms part of the environment. Their design and usage must serve the full participation of the assembly in its prayer.

2. Vessels should denote their function and invite participation. Engage artists and craftspersons in the creation of all appointments and vessels for liturgy that they might be authentic and beautiful objects with which we pray.

3. The tabernacle is not a focal point of any liturgy. It better serves its function when placed in a separate eucharistic chapel.

4. Vestments have a ministerial function. Their texture, shape, and colour gather the assembly's visual attentiveness for prayer.

5. Visual art has some supportive relationship to the actions that occur around it. Art is never mere decoration or display.

Discussion Questions

1. What ritual actions surround various books used in your worship? What attitudes do those actions convey about relationships in the church? about our relationship with God?

2. What attitudes are conveyed by the vessels you use for bread, wine, oil?

3. If you could re-design your liturgical vessels what materials and shapes would best combine simplicity, stewardship of resources, beauty and a sense of the holy?

4. As a liturgy committee share attitudes and experiences surrounding the tabernacle that you can remember from childhood to present day. How has your thinking changed? What might change in the future?

5. Discuss why lay persons should or should not wear albs when they preside.

Embodying the Paschal Mystery

To prepare liturgy is to make ready the coming of the Lord among us. Eternally Christ makes the passage from death to life in all creation. This movement is the paschal mystery that we celebrate at every liturgy, whatever the rite, whatever the time.

The paschal mystery is the energy that gives momentum to our lives day in and day out. In the ups and downs of relationships with friends, spouses, children and co-workers; in delightful moments of wonder and play; in the hard work of pursuing insight and truth about the world around us; in the sacrifices of responsible decisions and actions; in the yearnings of the human spirit that open us to the love of another, and the affection of God: in these paschal movements of the heart and of the universe, Christ passes over death and rises to new life in us.

When we celebrate liturgy in the ritual performance of gestures, music, words and symbols we embody our share in the paschal mystery of Jesus Christ. Giving flesh to our prayer in ritual is like embodying our love for a close friend with gestures of affection. The embodiment lets the mystery of love grow in us. Embodied love becomes the reality in which we live and move and have our being.

Embodying this mystery is what preparing the liturgical environment is all about. We prepare symbols, gestures, words and every sensate element that persons might experience in them the mystery of God among us. We don't control God's movement in our lives, but we can become present to its rhythms. When we make ready our Christian rituals, we prepare to be attentive with our whole selves—body, mind and spirit—that we might hear, see, smell, taste and touch God's presence.

GLOSSARY

Altar table: the table for eucharist is both altar, for our sacrifice of praise, and table, for our eucharistic meal.

Ambo: the privileged place from which the scriptures are read and the psalm sung. Not used for announcements. Other lecterns should appear to be less important.

Ambry: small cabinet, near the baptismal pool, for the attractive presentation of holy oils used in rituals of inititiation and anointing.

Apse: in a church fashioned after an oblong basilica,the semi-circular vaulted area that encloses the sanctuary.

Baptismal pool: plentiful flowing water is the full expression of baptism's primary symbol. As such the rites of inititiation are better served with a pool than a small bowl.

Environment: conflation of symbols, sensate experiences and physical space that embodies the assembly's ritual prayer.

Narthex: the gathering place or vestibule leading to the nave of the church. As a place of transition, requires deliberate planning.

Nave: the main part of the interior of the church in which people worship. Its liturgical function is to gather persons and enable members of the assembly to perform their ritual actions.

Sanctuary: customarily a stage-like platform at the front of a church, often thought of as the holy of holies. Can be renovated to reflect better the holiness of the entire people of God. The placement and design of the altar table, ambo, and presider's chair as focal points for common action, rather than objects for passive viewing, will facilitate the faithful's ministry as active participants at worship.

Symbol: visual image, sound, smell, taste, or tactile experience that evokes a feeling or is evoked by a feeling.

Tabernacle: from the Latin for "tent"; box used to safeguard the consecrated eucharistic bread. Also provides a repository for the blessed sacrament before which persons can pray privately. As such, a devotional object, not a liturgical focus. Therefore, can be located in a chapel away from the main worship space.

BIBLIOGRAPHY

Recommended Reading

Boyer, Mark G. *The Liturgical Environment. What the Documents Say.* Collegeville, MN: The Liturgical Press, 1991.

Federation of Diocesan Liturgical Commissions. *The Mystery of Faith: A Study of the Structural Elements of the Order of Mass* (revised edition). Washington: FDLC, 401 Michigan Ave. N.E., P.O. Box 29039, Washington, D.C. 20017, 1994.

Fischer, Edward. *Everybody Steals From God.* Notre Dame, Indiana: University of Notre Dame Press, 1977.

Hoffman, Elizabeth, ed. *The Liturgy Documents,* Third Edition. Chicago: Liturgy Training Publications, 1991. Includes, along with others, the *Constitution on the Sacred Liturgy,* the *General Instruction of the Roman Missal,* and the United States Catholic Conference of Bishops' document, *Environment and Art in Catholic Worship.*

Kavanagh, Aidan. *Elements of Rite.* New York: Pueblo Publishing Co., 1982; Collegeville, MN: The Liturgical Press, 1990.

Mauck, Marchita. *Shaping a House for the Church.* Chicago: Liturgy Training Publications, 1990.

Mazar, Peter. *To Crown the Year. Decorating the Church through the Seasons.* Chicago: Liturgy Training Publications, 1995.

McNorgan, David. "Non-verbal Dimensions of the Eucharist," *National Bulletin on Liturgy,* vol. 22, no. 118, September 1989.

Ross, Susan A. "The Aesthetic and the Sacramental," *Worship,* vol. 59, no. 1, Jan. 1985, 2-17.

Searle, Mark. "Liturgy as Metaphor," *Worship,* vol. 55, no. 2, March 1981, 98-119.

Searle, Mark. "Ritual & Music: A Theory of Liturgy and Implications for Music," *Assembly,* February 1986.

Simons, Thomas G. and Fitzpatrick, James M. *The Ministry of Liturgical Environment*. Collegeville, MN: The Liturgical Press, 1984.

Worgul, George S. *From Magic to Metaphor*. New York: Paulist Press, 1980.

Xavier, John Seubert. "Ritual Embodiment: Embellishment or Epiphany," in *Worship*, vol. 63, no. 5, Sept. 1989, 402-416.

imprimerie gagné ltée